# AFRICAN SAFARI TRIP

A GUIDED ACTIVITY JOURNAL by CARLY HEYWARD

ILLUSTRATED by COLLEEN FINN

ISBN: 979-8-989-3176-2-2

# THIS JOURNAL BELONGS TO

_____

## TRAVEL DATES

_____  —  _____

# HELPFUL WEBSITES!

### Uber

Many countries in Africa have Uber, so you can still use before you go. But confirm depending on which country you are going to.

### Stuarts' African Mammals

This is a paid app, but is an incredible resource

### Xe.com

A great website/app for currency conversion for any currency.

### iTrack Africa Lite

If you want to feel like a real spotter, this is a great way to start identifying any tracks you see. Especially if you see them in pics later and don't have your guide to ask.

### Merlin Bird ID

This app will help you figure out what bird you saw!

### FlightoftheEducator.com

I'm biased as I've made this journal to enhance your trip, but this is my blog! It has articles about what I spend on trips to help you plan yours, places to see in a country beyond the major tourist destinations, reviews of tours, and of course, my travel agent services should you like to utilize them.

SCAN TO GET MY PACKING LIST SUGGESTIONS!

# instructions

**This book is yours to write and draw in. Color, paste, add photos and use it however you'd like to document your Safari!**

# ABOUT ME!

I'm Carly Heyward, and I'm a former teacher turned travel agent. I specialize in Wildlife Expeditions to Antarctica, Galapagos and African Safaris.

Feel free to check out my blogs about my African Safaris and trips to over 90 countries, or if you'd like some personal help planning your own safari.

carly@flightoftheeducator.com

*Flight of the Educator*
Navigating the World on a Teacher's Budget

# Our Route

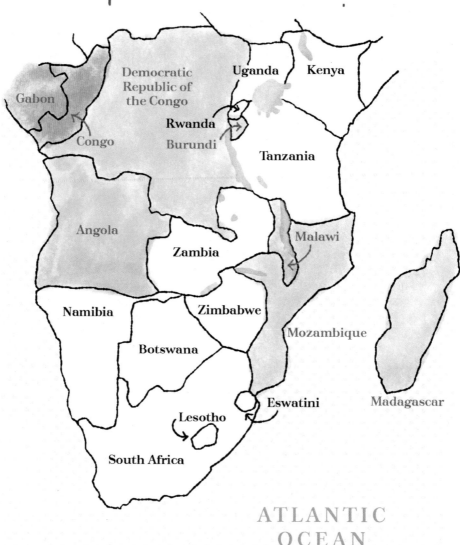

Gabon

Democratic
Republic of
the Congo

Uganda

Kenya

Congo

Rwanda

Burundi

Tanzania

Angola

Zambia

Malawi

Namibia

Zimbabwe

Mozambique

Botswana

Lesotho

Eswatini

Madagascar

South Africa

ATLANTIC
OCEAN

☆ WHY ARE YOU TAKING THIS TRIP?

☆ WHO ARE YOU TRAVELING WITH?

☆ WHAT ARE YOU LOOKING FORWARD
TO THE MOST?

# SAFARI
## - fun facts -

Over 3,000 languages are spoken in Africa with Arabic the most common.

The Masai people of Kenya think seeing a Buzzard in the morning is good luck.

You can make paper from Elephant and Rhino poop.

Boma is a Swahili word that means an enclosure used to protect a herd of animals or a camp.

Kruger is the largest game reserve in Africa. (Slightly smaller than Belgium)

Safari means Journey in Swahili.

Prey animals hang around giraffes because they provide early warning of predators.

Africa has over 25% of the world's bird species.

Elephants can be left or right "handed." Their preferred side's tusk will be shorter from extra use.

Johannesburg, South Africa is the most visited city in Africa.

# MIGRATION

The Great Migration takes place every year. It is a circular pattern the animals follow that goes over 1800 miles.

KENYA

TANZANIA

MASAI MARA NATIONAL RESERVE

AUGUST - OCTOBER

Thompson's Gazelle, Grant's Gazelle, Zebra, Wildebeest, and Eland are the only species that take part in the Great Migration.

NORTHERN SERENGETI

Zebra have good eyesight and Wildebeest have good hearing. With that, and since Zebra prefer tall grass and Wildebeest prefer short, they're perfect traveling companions.

JULY

NOVEMBER -DECEMBER

SERENGETI NATIONAL PARK

APRIL -JUNE

JANUARY -MARCH

NGORONGORO CONSERVATION AREA

MASAWA GAME RESERVE

They are constantly looking for fresh grazing and save the nutrient-rich (Thanks to volcanoes) grass for right before giving birth.

It helps with seed dispersal which helps the grass.

# COLLECTIVE NOUNS

A COLLECTIVE NOUN is a TERM
USED FOR a GROUP OF MANY
OF THE SAME KIND OF ANIMALS

A. Troop of _____.

B. Cloud of _____.

C. Obstinancy/Herd of _____.

D. Coalition of _____.

E. Bask of _____.

F. Parade of _____.

G. Flamboyance of _____.

H. Tower/Journey of _____.

I. Raft of _____.

| | | |
|---|---|---|
| CROCODILES | BATS | CHEETAHS |
| WILDEBEEST | ZEBRAS | PORCUPINES |
| LIONS | HYENAS | HIPPOS |
| MEERKATS | BUFFALO | FLAMINGOES |
| BABOONS | WARTHOGS | ELEPHANTS |
| GIRAFFES | LEOPARDS | RHINOS |

J. Cackle of _____.

K. Leap of _____.

L. Pride of _____.

M. Prickle of _____.

N. Crash of _____.

O. Dazzle of _____.

P. Implausibility of _____.

Q. Sounder of _____.

R. Mob of _____.

Troop of Baboons, Cloud of Bats, Obstinancy/herd of Buffalo, Coalition of Cheetahs, Bask of Crocodiles, Parade of Elephants, Flamboyance of Flamingoes, Tower/Journey of Giraffes, Raft of Hippos, Cackle of Hyenas, Leap of Leopards, Pride of Lions, Prickle of Porcupines, Crash of Rhinos, Dazzle of Zebras, Implausibility of Wildebeest, Sounder of Warthogs, Mob of Meerkats.

# CAMOUFLAGE

Camouflage is a tactic that animals use to avoid detection. Prey use it to avoid getting eaten and predators use it to avoid spooking their prey!

**PLAINS**

**MOUNTAIN**

**GREVY'S**

- For temperature control
- To provide a "fingerprint" for the young foals to imprint on
- To protect against flies
- To confuse lions, which choose an individual to hunt

- Called rosettes
- Break up the shape of the leopard in shadows
- Rosettes are dark with lighter center, or they can have smaller spots

ANGOLAN

RETICULATED

SOUTH AFRICAN

MASAI

- Primarily for comouflage
- Large blood vessels circle the patches, which regulate their body heat
- Skin under the patches have more sweat glands

ROTHSCHILD'S

# 'FOLLOW ME' MARKINGS

Most camouflage is designed to hide animals, however there are some markings on animals called "Follow Me" that allow animals to keep track of each other when following each other.

Black markings behind big cats' ears

impala tail down

white tail up when running away

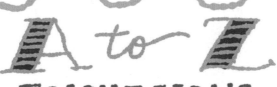

## EXCURSIONS

A _____

B _____

C _____

D _____

E _____

F _____

G _____

H _____

I _____

J _____

K _____

L _____

M _____

WRITE DOWN AN ANIMAL OR EXPERIENCE
YOU HAD FOR EACH OF THE LETTERS!
YOU MIGHT HAVE TO GET CREATIVE WITH SOME!

N _____

O _____

P _____

Q _____

R _____

S _____

T _____

U _____

V _____

W _____

X _____

Y _____

Z _____

# ANIMAL
# BINGO

TRY AND GO FOR BLACKOUT!
YOU CAN COLOR THE BLOCKS IN AS YOU DO THEM!

| | | | | |
|---|---|---|---|---|
| Lion | Porcupine | Mongoose | Vervet Monkey | Hippopotamus |
| Warthog | Giraffe | Crocodile | Guinea Fowl | Buffalo |
| Waterbuck | Bat | Leopard | Hyena | Impala |
| Baboon | Zebra | Wild Dog | Elephant | Cheetah |
| Rhino | Lilac Breasted Roller | Meerkat | Jackal | Kudu |

# EXPERIENCE

# BINGO

### TRY AND GO FOR BLACKOUT!
### YOU CAN COLOR THE BLOCKS IN AS YOU DO THEM!

| | | | | |
|---|---|---|---|---|
| Witnessed a Hunt | Giraffes Ate from a Tree | Saw a Baby Elephant | Someone Sang a Lion King Song | Leopard in Tree |
| Someone Said Hakuna Matata Unironically | Saw a Baby Big Cat | Went on a Night Safari | Met a Local | Saw an Animal's "Follow Me" Markings in Action |
| Dramatic Sunrise/ Sunset | Heard Elephant Trumpet | Saw a Dazzle of Zebras Running | Animal Walked by Vehicle | Swam in an Infinity Pool |
| Heard a Lion Roar | Referenced a Movie in Africa | Animal Road Block | Big Animal Yawned | Tracker Pointed out Tracks |
| Hot Air Balloon or Helicopter Ride | Sleeping Big Cat | Spotted a Well-Camouflaged Animal | Woke up Before the Sun | Saw a Cheetah Sprint |

# Animal Checklist

NOT ALL OF THESE ANIMALS WILL BE FOUND ON ALL safaris or areas, AND THERE are <u>more</u> animals THAN THIS!

## BIG FIVE
- ☐ Lion
- ☐ Leopard
- ☐ Rhino
- ☐ Elephant
- ☐ Buffalo

## LITTLE FIVE
- ☐ Ant Lion
- ☐ Leopard Tortoise
- ☐ Rhinoceros Beetle
- ☐ Elephant Shrew
- ☐ Buffalo Weaver

## HERBIVORES
- ☐ Giraffe
- ☐ Zebra
- ☐ Hippopotamus
- ☐ Warthog

## PRIMATES
- ☐ Baboon
- ☐ Vervet Monkey
- ☐ Chimpanzee
- ☐ Gorilla

## FELINES
- ☐ Cheetah
- ☐ African Wild Cat
- ☐ Caracal
- ☐ Serval

## CANINES
- ☐ African Wild Dog
- ☐ Jackal
- ☐ Hyena

## OTHER MAMMALS

- [ ] Honey Badger
- [ ] Civet
- [ ] Genet
- [ ] Pangolin
- [ ] Meerkat
- [ ] Porcupine
- [ ] Mongoose
- [ ] Bat
- [ ] Tree Squirrel
- [ ] Hare
- [ ] Hyrax

## ANTELOPE FAMILY

- [ ] Oryx
- [ ] Impala
- [ ] Kudu
- [ ] Nyala
- [ ] Waterbuck
- [ ] Duiker
- [ ] Sable Antelope
- [ ] Klipspringer
- [ ] Wildebeest
- [ ] Roan Antelope
- [ ] Eland

## REPTILES

- [ ] Crocodile
- [ ] Monitor
- [ ] Skink
- [ ] Terrapin

## BIRDS

- [ ] Vulture
- [ ] Ostrich
- [ ] Flamingo
- [ ] Secretary
- [ ] Egyptian Goose
- [ ] Kingfisher
- [ ] Guineafowl
- [ ] Eagle
- [ ] Owl
- [ ] Stork
- [ ] Crane
- [ ] Lilac Breasted Roller
- [ ] Nightjar
- [ ] Hornbill
- [ ] Stork
- [ ] Hamerkop

# The BIG FIVE

### Lion
**Kenya, Botswana, Tanzania, South Africa, Nambia, Zambia, and Zimbabwe**

Lions start off with small spots which fade away. They also like to hunt during storms. Their roar can be heard almost 5 miles away!

NOTES:

### Leopard
**Kenya, Botswana, Tanzania, South Africa, Namibia, Zambia, and Zimbabwe**

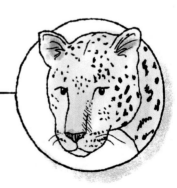

They are the most widely spread big cat in Africa. Leopards also like to bring their prey up in trees to eat them.

NOTES:

### Rhino
South Africa, Namibia,
Zimbabwe and Kenya

Their horns are made out of
keratin (just like your fingernails!).
NOTES:

### Elephant
Botswana, Zimbabwe, Tanzania,
Kenya, Namibia, Zambia,
and South Africa

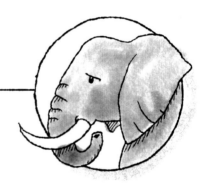

Elephants can "hear" with their feet!
NOTES:

### Cape Buffalo
Botswana, Zimbabwe, Tanzania,
Kenya, Namibia, Zambia,
and South Africa

They're sometimes called
"The Mafia" because of their
habit of taking revenge.
NOTES:

# The *little* FIVE

~~~~~~~~~~~~~~~~~~~~~~~~~~

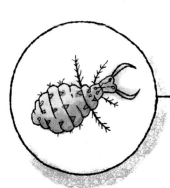

### Ant Lion
Sub-Saharan Africa

The larva mostly eat ants trapped in their sand pits, but the adults can fly.

NOTES:

### Leopard Tortoise
Sub-Saharan Africa

They're the 4th largest tortoise.

NOTES:

### Rhinoceros Beetle
Sub-Saharan Aftrica

They can lift 850 times their weight.

NoTes:

### Elephant Shrew
Sub-Saharan Africa

They can run almost 18 mph!

NoTes:

### Buffalo Weaver
Eastern and Southern Africa

They are exceptional nest builders, and they raise young as a community..

NoTes:

# The Ugly FIVE

### Warthog
Sub-Saharan Africa

They usually steal their burrows rather than make their own.

NOTES:

### Hyena
Ethiopia, Kenya, Tanzania, Botswana, South Africa & more

Their poop is white because of the calcium left in bones they eat.

NOTES:

### Marabou Stork
Sub-Saharan Africa

It uses its poop like sunscreen for its legs.

NOTES:

### Lappet-Faced Vulture
Kenya, Tanzania, Botswana, South Africa & more

Its stomach acid is so powerful that it can dissolve bones and kill pathogens that would make other animals sick.

NOTES:

### Wildebeest
Kenya, Tanzania, Botswana, South Africa & more

When calves are born, within minutes they can already run up to 40 mph.

NOTES:

# HERBIVORES

### Giraffe
Southern or Eastern Africa

Giraffes have adaptations for fighting gravity to move blood vertically, and scientists use that information as inspiration for space suits.

NoTes:

### Zebra
Southern or Eastern Africa

Zebras have a kick strong enough to kill a lion (sometimes).

NoTes:

### Hippopotamus
Sub-Saharan Africa

Hippos secrete a "blood sweat" which is a reddish, oily substance that they use as both sunscreen and antibacterial protection.

NoTes:

# PRIMATES

### Vervet Monkey
Eastern and Southeastern Africa

They have bright blue
male privates.

NOTES:

### Chimpanzee
West and Central Africa

They use tools such as sticks to
extract termites from mounds
and stones to crack open nuts.

NOTES:

### Baboon
Various regions across Africa

Adult male baboons have canine
teeth longer than those of a
leopard, which they display in
yawns to assert dominance.

NOTES:

# FELINES

### Cheetah
Sub-Saharan Africa

Named from a Hindi word "chita" which means "spotted one."

NoTes:

### Serval
Sub-Saharan Africa

They can jump up to 10 feet in the air!

NoTes:

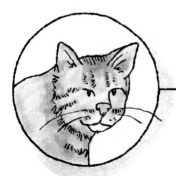

### African Wild Cat
All over Africa

They are the ancestors of domestic cats, with domestication believed to have started around 9,000 years ago.

NoTes:

# CANINES

### Jackal
Various regions of Africa

Jackals are monogamous and often hunt in pairs, coordinating their efforts to catch prey.

NOTES:

### African Wild Dog
Eastern and Southern Africa

African wild dogs have an 80% hunting success rate, one of the highest among predators, due to their cooperative pack strategies.

NOTES:

### Fox
Southern and Eastern Africa

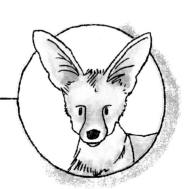

Their large ears not only provide excellent hearing but also help dissipate heat to regulate body temperature.

NOTES:

# ·OTHER·
# MAMMALS

## Honey Badger
### Sub-Saharan Africa

Honey badgers are known for their fearless nature and thick, rubbery skin almost 6 mm thick!

NOTES:

## Pangolin
### Across Africa

Name is from the Malay word "penggulung" which means roller. Its entire body is covered in scales that it rolls up into as an armored ball.

NOTES:

## Meerkat
### Southern Africa

They decide the next matriarch with an "eating contest." They want the heaviest female!

NOTES:

### Porcupine
Across Africa

The Cape porcupine is the
largest rodent in Africa,
growing up to a meter long
and weighing up to 44 lbs.

NOTES:

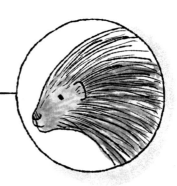

### Mongoose
Across Africa

They've been seen using tools
like rocks to crack open eggs.

NOTES:

### Bat
Across Africa

They are the only flying mammal!

NOTES:

# ANTELOPES

### Antelope
#### Across Africa

There are nearly 100 different species of antelope.

NOTES:

### Gazelle
#### Across Africa

Gazelles don't outrun cheetahs; they outmaneuver them, including using a move called "Pronking."

NOTES:

### Impala
#### Eastern and Southern Africa

Impalas are exceptional jumpers, able to leap distances of up to 33 feet and heights of 10 feet.

NOTES:

### Kudu
Eastern and Southern Africa

They have the longest horns of any antelope. They can be up to 6 feet long!

NoTes:

### Nyala
Southern Africa

They're the most sexually dysmorphic, and they also hang out under trees that baboons and monkeys are in to eat the fruit they drop.

NoTes:

### Waterbuck
Sub-Saharan Africa

They're most known for their toilet seat marking on their backside.

NoTes:

### Oryx
Eastern and Southern Africa

Oryxes can survive without water for a long time, getting moisture from the plants and minimizing water loss through specialized physiological adaptations.

NoTes:

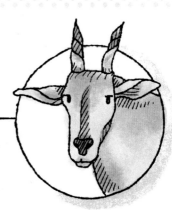

### Eland
Southern Africa

They're the largest antelope (up to 2200 lbs!), but can still jump over 4 feet from a standstill.

NoTes:

### Duiker
Sub-Saharan Africa

Duikers known for their shy behavior and ability to dive into thick vegetation when threatened, a trait that inspired their name, which means "diver" in Afrikaans.

NoTes:

# REPTILES

### Crocodile
#### Sub-Saharan Africa

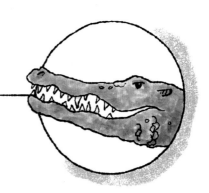

Nile crocodiles have the strongest
bite force of any animal,
capable of exerting a force eight
times more powerful than that
of a great white shark.

NOTES:

### Monitor
#### Across Africa

They can eat 5.5 lbs of food
in one minute!

NOTES:

### Terrapin
#### Across Africa

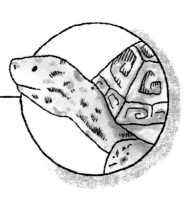

They use their long necks to
flip themselves back upright!

NOTES:

# BIRDS

### Ostrich
Across Africa

The ostrich is the world's largest bird and can run at speeds up to 45 mph.

NºTES:

### Flamingo
Along the Coasts of Africa

They can fly over 300 miles, 50-60 mph, and up to 15,000 feet!

NºTES:

### Secretary
Sub-Saharan Africa

Despite having almost a 6 ft wingspan, they don't fly much. They use their powerful kicks to hunt. Often snakes, but have been seen to attack even baby cheetahs and gazelles.

NºTES:

### Hornbill
Across Africa

Some hornbill species' females seal themselves inside a tree cavity using mud and remain there throughout incubation and chick-rearing, relying on the male to provide food.

NoTes:

### Lilac Breasted Roller
Southern Africa

It's the national bird of Kenya! And they use brush fires to easily find their prey escaping the fire.

NoTes:

### Guineafowl
Sub-Saharan Africa

They are strong flyers, but they still often prefer to run, even to escape predators.

NoTes:

# WHAT A TRIP!

☆ WHAT WAS THE MOST EXCITING PART?

☆ DESCRIBE AN INTERESTING PERSON YOU MET.

☆ WHO WAS YOUR FAVORITE SAFARI GUIDE? WHY?

☆ WHAT DID YOU DO ON YOUR DOWNTIME?

The rest of the book is yours to document your trip as you see fit! The opposite page is an example of what it could look like - but also open for you to chronicle your journey however you'd like.

Here are some inspirations of different things you could include!

- **Daily trip log (temp, weather, what you did & highlights)**

- **First impressions**

- **Wildlife encounters**

- **Landscape and scenery**

- **Weather**

- **Food**

- **General reflections**

- **Funny stories**

- **What did you learn**

- **Photographs & memories**

- **Experiences with food, lodges, people**

- **Personal growth**

- **Gratitudes**

Made in the USA
Coppell, TX
18 June 2025

50857916R00031